Our Bodies

Our Stomachs

Charlotte Guillain

Heinemann Library
Chicago, Illinois

www.heinemannraintree.com
Visit our website to find out
more information about
Heinemann-Raintree books.

To order:
☎ Phone 888-454-2279
💻 Visit www.heinemannraintree.com
to browse our catalog and order online.

Editorial: Rebecca Rissman, Laura Knowles, Nancy Dickmann,
  and Sian Smith
Picture research: Ruth Blair and Mica Brancic
Designed by Joanna Hinton-Malivoire
Original Illustrations © Capstone Global Library Ltd. 2010
Illustrated by Tony Wilson
Printed and bound by Leo Paper Group

14 13 12 11 10
10 9 8 7 6 5 4 3 2 1

Library of Congress Cataloging-in-Publication Data
Guillain, Charlotte.
  Our stomachs / Charlotte Guillain.
     p. cm. -- (Our bodies)
  Includes bibliographical references and index.
  ISBN 978-1-4329-3591-7 (hc) -- ISBN 978-1-4329-3600-6 (pb)
  1. Stomach--Juvenile literature. 2. Digestion--Juvenile literature.
  I. Title.
  QP151.G85 2010
  612.3'2--dc22
                                          2009022295

Acknowledgments
The author and publisher are grateful to the following for
permission to reproduce copyright material:
© Capstone Global Library pp.**16**, **17** (Karon Dubke); Corbis p.**19**
(© ROB & SAS); iStockphoto pp.**18** (© Rob Friedman), **20** (© Elena
Elisseeva); Photolibrary pp.**4** (© Goodshoot), **5** (© Banana Stock), **8** (©
Fancy), **9** (© 4x5 Coll-Paul Simcock/Superstock), **10** (© Stockbyte), **21**
(© Brand X Pictures), **22** (© Banana Stock); Science Photo Library p.**12**
(© Alfred Pasieka); Shutterstock pp.**13** (© Stephen Mcsweeny), **14** (©
NatashaBo).

Front cover photograph of a girl picking an apple reproduced with
permission of Corbis (© Rolf Brenner). Back cover photograph
reproduced with permission of Photolibrary (© Stockbyte).

Every effort has been made to contact copyright holders of any
material reproduced in this book. Any omissions will be rectified in
subsequent printings if notice is given to the publisher.

Contents

Body Parts

Our bodies have many parts.

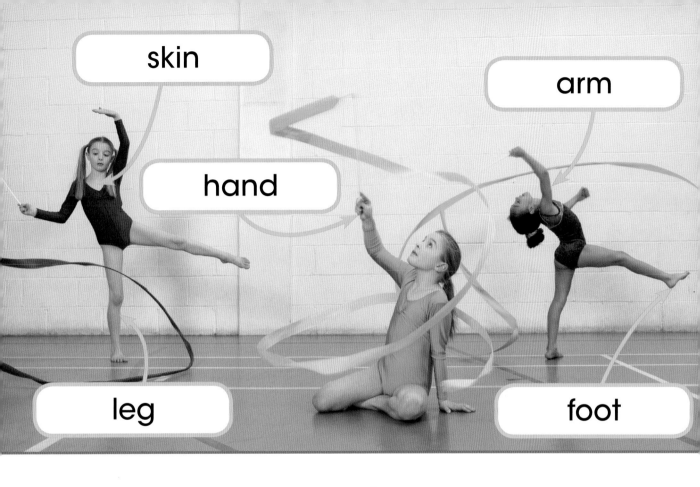

skin

arm

hand

leg

foot

Our bodies have parts on
the outside.

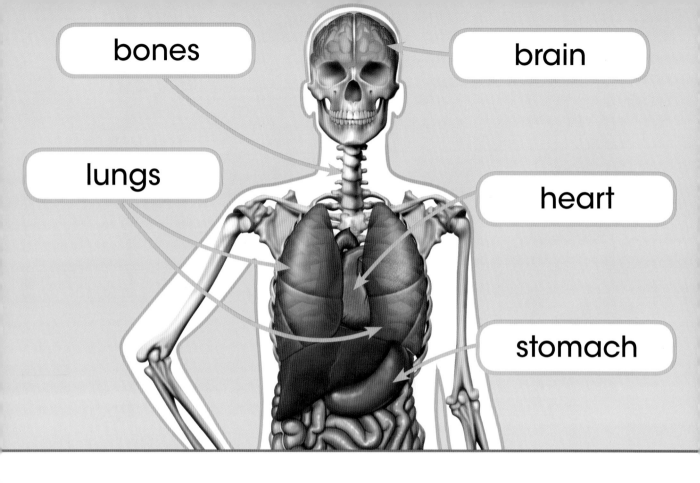

bones

brain

lungs

heart

stomach

Our bodies have parts on
the inside.

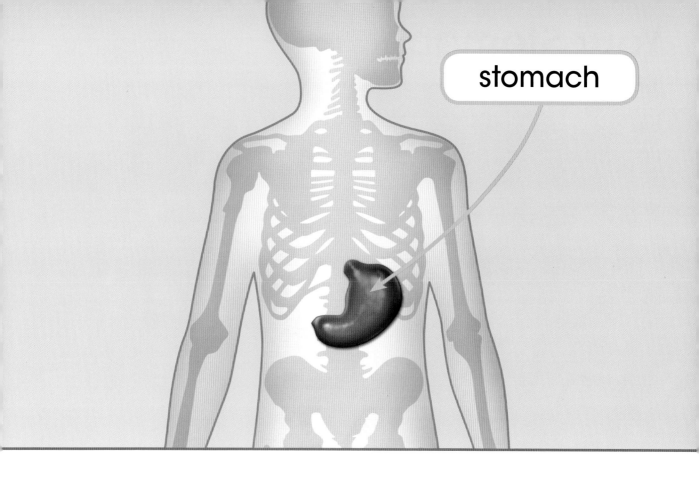

Your stomach is inside your body.

Your Stomach

You cannot see your stomach.

stomach

Your stomach is inside your body.

Eating

mouth

You eat with your mouth.

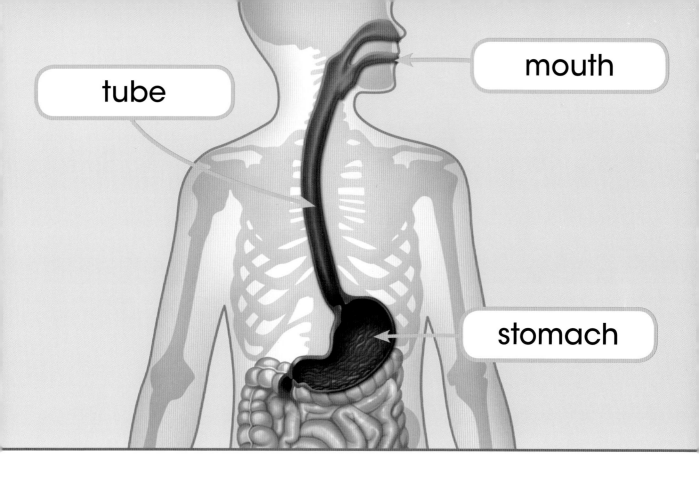

tube

mouth

stomach

A tube goes from your mouth to
your stomach.

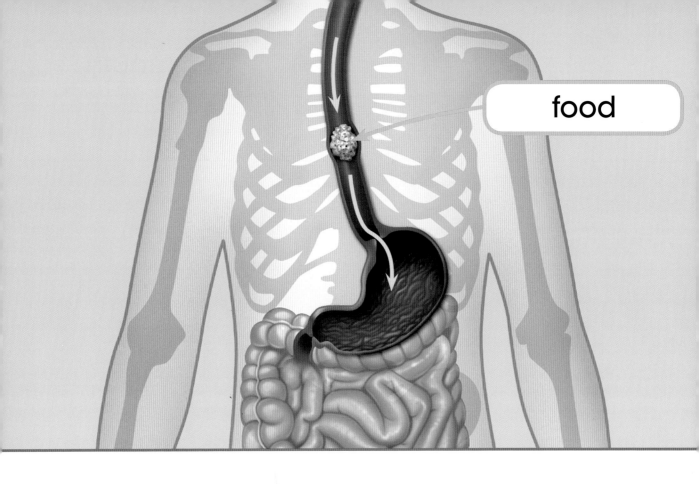

food

Food goes into your stomach.

Drinks go into your stomach, too.

Your stomach holds food like
a bag.

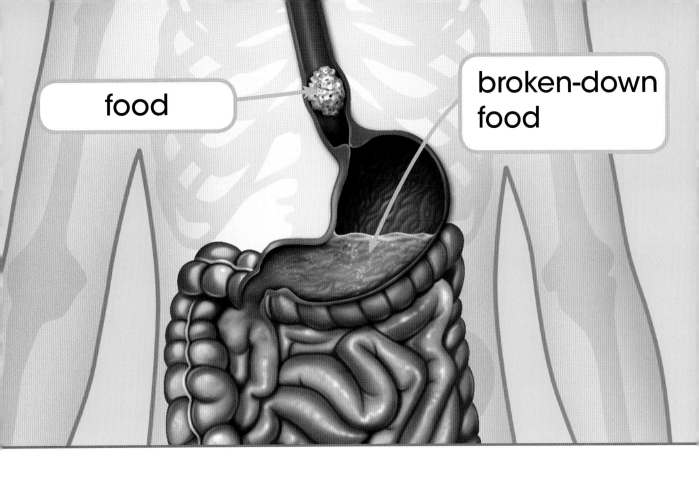

food

broken-down food

Your stomach breaks down the food.

Full and Empty

You can feel when your stomach is full.

Sometimes your stomach hurts when it is full.

You can feel when your stomach
is empty.

Sometimes your stomach makes
sounds when it is empty.

Staying Healthy

You can drink plenty of water to help your stomach.

You can eat healthy food to help your stomach.

Quiz

Where in your body is
your stomach?

 22

Answer on page 24

Picture Glossary

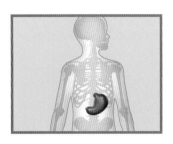

stomach part of your body that breaks food into tiny bits so that your body can use it

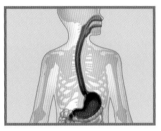

tube a long, thin pipe like a hose. Things can move through tubes because they have an empty space in the middle.

Index

Answer to quiz on page 22: Your stomach is inside your body.

Notes to parents and teachers
Before reading
Ask children to name the parts of their body they can see on the outside. Then ask them what parts of their body are inside. Make a list of them together and see if the children know what each body part does, for example, they need their lungs to breathe. Discuss where their stomach is and ask if anyone knows what stomachs do.

After reading
• Put children into groups and give each group a balloon and a funnel. Tell them that the flat balloon is like their stomachs when they are empty. Then ask them to use the funnel to slowly pour water into the balloon. Discuss how the balloon is stretching in the same way our stomachs stretch when we eat and drink.